Original title:
Nettle Notes

Copyright © 2025 Creative Arts Management OÜ
All rights reserved.

Author: Eleanor Prescott
ISBN HARDBACK: 978-1-80566-707-0
ISBN PAPERBACK: 978-1-80566-992-0

Beneath the Prickly Veil

In a garden where plants conspire,
Laughter blooms, never tires.
With leaves that tickle and tease,
Who knew weeds could be such a breeze?

A poke or jab, oh what a game,
Each prickly friend has a funny name.
Dancing in the sunlight's glow,
Watch your step, or you might go, whoa!

The Hidden Sting of Harmony

A chorus of greens, all sing in tune,
Though one sneaks up with a sharp balloon.
When gardening's a jolly fair,
Watch out! One's waiting in your hair!

With laughter mixed in earthy soil,
Nature serves up a poetic toil.
Harmonies that tickle your nose,
The hidden sting, oh how it glows!

Furrows of Foliage Friction

In rows where mischief tends to play,
Plants jostle about in a cheeky way.
Foliage fights with a playful jab,
Who knew greens could be so drab?

Tiny thorns with a wink of fun,
A sneaky laugh when day is done.
In this patch of fibrous cheer,
Every nick gives a reason to cheer!

The Rustle of Resilient Roots

Beneath the surface, a giggling spree,
Roots whisper secrets, quite amusingly.
Tangled tales under a laughing sky,
Nature's way of asking, 'Oh, my, why?'

A giddy sort of plant parade,
Each wobbly stem's a funny charade.
With rustles loud that catch the breeze,
Those resilient roots just aim to please!

The Allure of the Rough Path

I wandered down a tangled trail,
Where thorns and giggles play a tale.
Each prick comes with a secret laugh,
As nature draws its crooked path.

The crunch beneath my foolish feet,
Is nature's way of saying, 'beat!'.
With every scratch, a quirky glee,
Adventure calls, 'Come dance with me!'

Musings of the Stalks

Tall tales from the humble green,
Whispered gossip, quite the scene.
'Is that a frog or just a shoe?'
They giggle soft, while sipping dew.

With every sway in the gentle breeze,
They poke at clouds, and tease the trees.
In this odd court of leafy jest,
The stalks declare, 'We're simply the best!'

Green Graffiti of the Wilderness

Splashes of emerald, no fine art,
Nature's canvas, wild and smart.
Doodles made by buzzing bees,
With splatters bright among the leaves.

Each mark a giggle, each curl a wink,
The forest's jibe, too grand to think.
Graffiti of the earth's delight,
Painted by twinkling stars at night.

Embrace of the Wild Weeds

Hugs from leaves, so soft and bold,
In their twisty arms, a secret told.
With roots that tickle and stems that tease,
They wrap around, like a breeze with ease.

'Come join the party!' the clovers shout,
'We're here for fun, that's what it's about!'
In every leaf, a story sprawls,
As laughter echoes in quirk-filled halls.

The Unseen Kiss of Flora

In the garden, plants conspire,
Winking leaves that never tire.
With every brush, I sense a tease,
Nature's humor, like a breeze.

A flower whispers, quite a jibe,
"Watch your step, it's not a bribe!"
Prickly greens that nudge and poke,
In silence, they share a joke.

Cultivating the Unpredictable

Sowing seeds of sheer surprise,
Watch out for the playful lies!
One day blooms, the next a thorn,
It's a circus, nature's born.

Rabbits giggle, squirrels prance,
In this foliage, they take a chance.
Chasing shadows, things mislaid,
Every harvest, quite a charade.

The Art of Nature's Barbs

In the gallery of green and gold,
Artful prickers, brave and bold.
Crafted by the hands of time,
Nature's snippets, quite sublime.

A thistle's wink, a dandelion grin,
Inviting mischief to begin.
The spiny ones don't mind the jest,
A sharp retort, they do their best.

Green Enigmas in the Breeze

Leaves that dance with secret schemes,
Laughter hides in shadows' beams.
Rustling whispers, what could they mean?
A riddle wrapped in shades of green.

The breeze giggles, plays along,
In a world where prickers belong.
Finding joy in nature's quirks,
Life's a stage where humor lurks.

The Soul of the Overgrown Path

In a garden where weeds are kings,
Laughter bursts from tangled strings.
Beneath the green, a secret war,
The daisies giggle, wanting more.

Thorns are prancing, clumsy twirls,
While bug-eyed ants do little swirls.
A dandelion lost its puff,
"Who needs a haircut? No, that's tough!"

The moonlight dances on leafy feet,
As shadows play hide-and-seek, oh sweet!
A butterfly jokes with a ladybug,
"What's the buzz? Let's give a shrug!"

So wander down this path of cheer,
Where folly grows and friends appear.
With every step, the fun still blooms,
In this kingdom of playful rooms.

Dances of the Unseen Root

Beneath the surface, roots engage,
They twist and twirl, a tiny stage.
Whispers float on covert nights,
Mice on stilts pretend they're knights.

A wise old fern gives silly advice,
"To wear your leaves like fancy dice!"
Each sprout can't help but laugh and sing,
As rain drops fall—oh, what they bring!

The crabgrass does its wiggly dance,
Swaying 'round in a merry trance.
"Don't step here; instead, be brave,
Join us under the moonlit wave!"

There's joy hidden beneath the grime,
Where laughter grows and sprouts with time.
So shake a root, embrace the fun,
In the wild game that's never done!

Rhymes Beneath the Underbrush

In shadows where mischief thrives,
Whiskered critters give high-fives.
A caterpillar lost the show,
"Who needs wings? I'm still a pro!"

Moss is soft like a dreamer's bed,
While frogs recite with wit so spread.
"Oh dear snail, you're slow, it's true,
But look at me! My shell's askew!"

A trio of toads croak out a tune,
With a silly frog-leap, they swoon.
The brambles chuckle, soft and sly,
"Dance with us—let fancies fly!"

So creeping through these leafy lanes,
The air is filled with playful strains.
What joy lies low within the brush,
Where laughter touches every hush!

Whimsy in the Wild Greenery

The tall grass sways with a cheeky grin,
While squirrels start their acorn spin.
A blossom shouts, "It's time to play!"
As bees bring jokes to brighten the day.

A hedgehog rolls, a tumbleweed,
"Oh, what a sight! It's my I-can't-breed!"
With laughter blossoming everywhere,
The flowers high-five with a colorful flair.

The wind whispers tales of nutty delight,
"Join our party under starlight!"
A wild song hums through the leafy throng,
Where every mishap seems to belong.

So come and join this garden spree,
With giggles sprouting from every tree.
In wild greenery, fun takes its chance,
Where whimsy waltzes and all things prance!

Nature's Cautionary Song

In the garden where I tread,
Beware the prickly dance ahead.
They wave their arms, they shout and scream,
But who knew weeds could plot and scheme?

Lurking close, with stealthy glee,
A thistle grins, just wait and see.
It whispers tales of woe and dread,
Yet all I hear is 'ouch' instead!

With flowers sweet and colors bright,
Some plants will give you quite a fright.
Like jesters hiding in the brush,
They'll catch your leg and make you rush!

So heed the call of playful green,
For nature's art can be obscene.
Amidst the blooms, a warning clear:
Watch where you step, or gain a spear!

Tales Spun from Twisted Stems

There once was a flower, bold and grand,
Who danced in circles, quite unplanned.
With petals bright, it laughed in glee,
While tangled roots were plotting free.

The vines conspired, twisting tight,
Making a game of a gentle fright.
"Come closer!" they chimed, "don't hesitate!"
But laughter followed—was it too late?

A rogue dandelion dared to tease,
"Do you really think I'm just a breeze?"
It blew them backwards, oh what a sight,
As weeds chuckled loud, with sheer delight.

Oh tales from the earth, spun with fun,
A comedy show, a greenish run!
So when you stroll through nature's way,
Watch for giggles in the foliage play!

Vibrations of the Wild Flora

In fields where laughter echoes loud,
The flowers form their silly crowd.
Petals tickle, roots make a scene,
Who knew greens could be so mean?

With stems that sway to a tune so sweet,
Twirling and whirling, they can't be beat.
Yet as I dance and kick my feet,
A nettle strikes—oh what a feat!

"Join us now!" cries the daffodil,
As I stumble over with a thrill.
A thistle sings, "You've got the moves!"
But trust me, friend, it's a wild groove!

The wild flora giggles and croons,
As I dodge the barbs beneath the moons.
Vibrations of laughter fill the air,
Beware the plants that start to dare!

The Cauldron of Earthly Spells

In nature's pot, where mischief brews,
A cauldron bubbles with oddities and hues.
"Stir it well!" croaked the toad so wise,
"Add a pinch of thorns—what a surprise!"

A sprinkle of laughter, a dash of fright,
This potion's brewing into the night.
Watch out for petals, those jokesters sly,
They'll mix you up and make you fly!

Twisting roots, they twist and tease,
Making spells to bring you to your knees.
"Jump right in!" the daisies chide,
But in the mix, do not abide!

For every charm has a hidden twist,
An earthy prank you might have missed.
So dip your toes, but heed my tale,
In the cauldron's brew, you might just wail!

Nature's Unforgiving Touch

In fields where green is bold and bright,
A tickle here can bring a fright.
With unsuspecting swipes of grass,
Nature's play can sting like sass.

A careless step, a playful dance,
Turns joy into a prickly trance.
With laughter mixed in every tear,
The garden's quirks, oh so sincere.

We braved the weeds, we took a chance,
A floral foe, a wild romance.
But who knew that a gentle brush,
Could lead to such a fiery rush!

So next time you walk where wild things grow,
Remember where those prickles show.
A funny tale of nature's ways,
Will surely last for many days.

The Sage of Stinging Secrets

A wise old sage with pricks of green,
Whispers secrets, sharply keen.
With every poke, a lesson learned,
In laughter's weave, his wisdom churned.

He speaks of joy found in the sting,
Of how the laughs from pain can spring.
In every ouch, a chuckle lies,
A way to see through teary eyes.

When wandering paths with tendrils wide,
They teach us well to turn the tide.
For what's a scratch but nature's joke?
A crafty quip from leafy folk.

So heed this sage, with wisdom clear,
And find the fun among the fear.
Nature's humor has a twist,
In every stinging scratch, don't miss!

Growth Spurred by Nature's Hand

In gardens lush where dangers creep,
The laughter grows, it runs so deep.
Each little sting, a friendly jest,
Nature's way of making zest.

When fingers dive into the green,
They often leave a stinging sheen.
A playful push, a hearty laugh,
Finding joy in nature's path.

Every scratch is just a tease,
A tickling touch from swaying trees.
With every pain, a growth begins,
Creating tales of chuckles and grins.

So trod with care, and mind the foe,
For what's a prick but fun on show?
The sprouting laughter never ends,
In nature's arms, we make our friends.

Wilderness Poems of Pain

Amidst the wild, the laughter rings,
With every scratch, a story stings.
The thorns that scratch are just a game,
In nature's play, there's no real shame.

The paths we tread are filled with cheer,
Though pricking pains may disappear.
A giggle follows every dare,
As nature's winks fill the air.

With humor gripped in every sway,
A funny twist to light our way.
Even in stings, we find delight,
In wilderness poems steeped in light.

So let us dance through prickly fields,
Embracing all that laughter yields.
With zany tales, our spirits soar,
In every poke, we ask for more.

The Texture of Green Whispers

In a garden where jokes take root,
Leaves giggle while the branches hoot.
A spider spins tales of wobbly dance,
While daisies join in a sunny prance.

The breeze tickles every cheek,
As butterflies share secrets unique.
Petals crack jokes, a flowery play,
Nature's laughter, brightening the day.

Blueprints of Natural Strife

Bees plot mischief with sticky plans,
While worms wiggle in their tiny bands.
A squirrel's stash of acorns and snacks,
Leads to hilarity with sneaky hacks.

Mice hold meetings to discuss their cheese,
Arguing over who runs fastest with ease.
Nature's chaos in every small critter,
Crafting a comedic dance, oh so bitter.

The Unruly Green Sonnet

A frog sings off-key by the lily pads,
And the fish all chuckle, it's simply mad.
The sun winks down at this foolish bard,
While a quacking duck plays the foil, the card.

Thistles argue with daisies, it's a roast,
Both claim they're the flower that blooms the most.
As the wind joins in with a playful shove,
It's nature's stand-up, filled with love.

Cadence of Cloudy Canopies

In treetops where shadows plot and scheme,
Leaves toss around their dreams like a dream.
Squirrels chase tails in a dizzying race,
While the owls hoot applause, keeping the pace.

Clouds drift by with messages unclear,
Whispering hints on the weather they hear.
A woodpecker laughs, tapping out a beat,
As forest life dances on nimble feet.

Chronicles of the Serpent's Kiss

In a garden, green and bright,
A serpent danced with sheer delight.
He twirled around, but what a sight,
He stumbled, oh! It gave a fright.

With every hiss, a giggle burst,
He snagged his tail, oh, that was cursed.
He tried to charm, but wholly missed,
And from the bushes came a twist.

The butterflies were in a flurry,
As the serpent darted, all in a hurry.
He slipped on dew, oh what a fuss,
Now covered in mud, not a bit of gloss.

But laughter rang through leafy boughs,
As creatures gathered, took their vows.
To skip and tumble, join this fun,
In the wild, they had all won.

Musings from the Untamed Realm

In a thicket, mischief brewed,
Where creatures gathered, all subdued.
A rabbit wore a tiny hat,
Declared a party, fancy that!

The fox, amused, brought snacks galore,
While owl could barely keep the score.
Dancing leaves, a breezy spin,
As critters twirled, let joy begin.

The hedgehog brought some prickly pies,
While squirrels laughed at their own highs.
With hiccups loud and giggles bright,
They reveled through the starry night.

But as the dawn began to glow,
A sleepy crowd, moved nice and slow.
"Till next time!" chirped the morning sun,
Leaving tales of laughter, pure fun.

Haiku of the Hidden Spine

In the grass they lie,
Worms wiggling, dance sublime,
Nature's sneak attack.

Curly tails in glee,
Sneaky wriggles, oh, so sly,
A tickle from the dew.

Underneath the bloom,
The creatures laugh and they play,
Hidden wonders sway.

The Touch of Nature's Caress

In a meadow wide and free,
Bumblebees buzzed happily.
With petals bright, they shared a joke,
As daisies danced and the sun awoke.

A worm complained about the rain,
While butterflies swooped, no time for pain.
The ladybug, in tiny shoes,
Strolled fashionably while spreading news.

The wind brought whispers through the leaves,
As laughter rippled 'neath tall eaves.
"Let's play a game!" the cricket said,
And all agreed, though some just fled.

With a hop, a skip, and a twirl,
Round and round, they gave a whirl.
In nature's heart, where fun's the plan,
They basked in joy, a blissful clan.

The Intimacy of Rough Edges

In the garden where whispers vie,
Thorns offer tales, oh my my!
In patchy hugs, we all convene,
With scratchy love best seen, not mean.

A poke, a jab, a laugh, a sigh,
These prickle puns just fly so high.
With every bend, a giggle's drawn,
In jagged jests, we stretch till dawn.

The prickly path, our crooked dance,
With merry banter, we take a chance.
Embracing flaws in silly jest,
A raucous joy, we love the quest.

The Art of Prickly Conversations

A chat begins with barbed intent,
As quips and jabs become our rent.
In sharp remarks, we find our glee,
  With each comical misanatomy.

Over tea, our laughter flows,
With every poke, humor grows.
The art of jest, our prickly style,
Brings radiant smiles, our thorny pile.

From curt replies to witty throngs,
We build our tales in stings and songs.
Each twisty line a crafty catch,
In fine-spun jest, we find our match.

Poetry in the Haunt of Thorns

In the thicket where shadows play,
We weave our rhymes in a prickly way.
Each verse a jab, each line a poke,
The laughter bursts, a joyous cloak.

What's that afoot? A snicker, a laugh,
In this twisted world, we cut our path.
Haikus with bites and limericks sharp,
In thorns' embrace, we find our spark.

With every sting, a tale to tell,
In a garden where giggles swell.
So grab a quill, and let it twine,
In this maze of mirth, we intertwine.

Hymn to the Silent Sentinel

Oh sentinel so stout and bold,
In silence, your stories unfold.
A twisted grin upon your face,
In your prickly arms, we find our space.

Through sunny days and stormy nights,
You stand and bear our fanciful flights.
A chorus of chuckles, a symphony sweet,
In the heart of thorns, we find our beat.

We dance around your jagged frame,
In every scratch, we roar your name.
For in this garden, weird and wild,
You teach us the heart of the silly child.

Fractals of the Feral Garden

In a patch of wild and whimsy,
Rabbits dance, quite unconvincingly.
Each bloom a surprise, a giggle blooms,
While bees lose their way in floral rooms.

A garden grows with no design,
Where tangled vines conspire to dine.
The zucchinis argue, 'We're the best!'
While carrots sulk, 'We're just a jest!'

Lettuce heads shake in disbelief,
As raindrops giggle, shaking grief.
The scarecrow snoozes, draped in flair,
Woken by a rebellious hare.

Yet amidst the chaos, joy remains,
In every poke and prod, the gains.
For laughter sprouts in every weed,
And nature's quirks plant light with speed.

The Poetry of Prickles

A porcupine pens a love note,
With quills that make the heart gloat.
Romance stings like a playful jest,
When spines can twist and still caress.

Cacti stand proud, with swagger and flare,
Claiming the desert, without a care.
Sun-soaked spines play hide and seek,
Finding laughter in the quirky peak.

The rose gives a wink, then a poke,
While the gardener chuckles at the joke.
For beauty comes wrapped in sharp delight,
In the world's garden, a comical sight.

So raise your glass to sharp-tongued friends,
In the poetry of life that never ends.
With humor sharp and smiles vast,
Let's toast to the moments, heartily cast!

Whispered Histories of the Field

In the field where shadows play,
Every blade has something to say.
A tale of mischief on breezy nights,
As mice duel in comical fights.

The corn whispers secrets of the past,
How the raccoon raided at last.
Each ear of grain holds giggly glee,
While the thistle witnesses with a tree!

Dandelions cheer for the sun's embrace,
While beetles race in a busy chase.
The field is a stage, a comedy grand,
Where every critter plays a hand.

So listen close to nature's cheer,
In whispered tales, the laughter's near.
For in the rustle, humor resides,
In every whisper, joy abides.

The Breath of the Bristling Woods

In forests filled with sprightly noise,
Squirrels scamper, the clumsy joys.
Branches rustle with secrets and jests,
While owls roll eyes as the raccoon quests.

The trees gossip, leaves in a flurry,
As foxes pretend, they're in a hurry.
Woodpeckers tap, their rhythm a beat,
In this wood of fun, a whimsical street.

Mushrooms giggle under their hats,
While hedgehogs waddle, engaging in chats.
A fairy watches with twinkling eyes,
As laughter echoes, beneath leafy skies.

The woods breathe mischief, wild and free,
With nature's antics, in every spree.
So stroll through the brambles, collect the light,
In the breath of the woods, find pure delight!

Musings of the Jagged Edge

In the garden where I tread,
Spiky whispers fill my head.
Every step, a giggle blooms,
As I dodge those prickly rooms.

Dancing plants with a sly grin,
Tickling toes under my skin.
I trip on roots, oh what a sight,
A comedy of nature's plight.

Wandering the wild today,
Silly thorns lead me astray.
Yet I laugh with every poke,
Nature's jest, and I'm the joke.

Beneath the sun, I find delight,
Inspite of every pricky bite.
The jagged edge of blissful cheer,
Is where I shed my every fear.

Chronicles from the Rugged Glen

In the glen where shadows roam,
I hear the giggles of my home.
Bouncing boughs like funny clowns,
Hiding mischief, wearing frowns.

Silly squirrels, a nutty band,
Plot their tricks with tiny hands.
Did you see them? Chasing tails,
While spinning wildly, off the trails.

Up the hill, the ruckus grows,
Thatch and thistle strike a pose.
With every snap, a laugh escapes,
In this place of wobbly shapes.

Even trees have tales to tell,
Of how they tripped and fell quite well.
As I wander, grins expand,
In the rugged glens, life's so grand.

Whispers of a Thistle Breeze

The breeze speaks softly, quick and light,
Woven whispers that spark delight.
Thistles laugh with a pokey jest,
In a dance that feels like a test.

With every gust, a flutter calls,
Tickling my nose, as laughter falls.
Nature's jesters, wild and free,
Spinning tales just for me.

Beside the path, the flowers play,
Colorful antics of the day.
They sway and bow with coy intent,
Unruly fun that's heaven-sent.

I join the dance, a silly spree,
With every prickle, more glee for me.
In this breeze where joy adheres,
Every poke brings sudden cheers.

Shadows of the Stinging Herb

In the twilight, shadows creep,
Among the herbs that never sleep.
With a twitch, they do conspire,
To set my cautious soul on fire.

Each step yields a cheeky poke,
I yelp aloud, oh what a joke!
The garden laughs at my distress,
As plants conspire in their mess.

I swear they're hiding naughty schemes,
Those lurking leaves, with scruffy dreams.
Beneath the moon, pranksters play,
Stinging giggles lead the way.

Yet still I tread, though cautious now,
With chuckles shared, here I bow.
In the presence of this herbal jest,
I find my sanity's at best.

Ripples of Wild Growth

In the garden where weeds laugh,
A flower sneezed, and then it chaffed.
The daisies dance, a comical sight,
While snails host races, oh what a fright!

A root poked out, a bumpy bump,
While ants held parties, they stomp and thump.
The butterflies giggle, fluttering so free,
As the carrots mock them, oh woe to be me!

Grapevines tangle in a wild embrace,
And twigs stick out in a messy place.
The garlic smells funny, like socks on a run,
In this whimsical patch, we all share the fun!

So here's to the chaos, the joy that it brings,
Each weed holds a story, with laughter it sings.
In the riot of greens, we find our delight,
In this tangled-up garden, everything's bright!

Touching the Prickled Skin

A brave little lass with bare feet did roam,
Stepping on thistles, she'd giggle and moan.
"Look at my toes!" she would playfully shout,
With a prickly surprise that nobody doubts.

Behind every leaf, mischief does hide,
With robins telling tales of their wild, swooping glide.
A hedgehog rolls by, its spines on full show,
"Oh dear!" she exclaims, "Don't sit on me, no!"

When the breeze blows softly, the garden takes flight,
With petals like confetti in sunshine so bright.
The prickles are tickles, a laugh and a jest,
In this quirky land, it's all for the best!

So if you should wander where wild things do play,
Be ready for laughter that brightens the day.
With joy in our hearts and some pricks on our skin,
We'll dance with the weeds, let the fun times begin!

Verses of the Bramble Way

In the thicket where brambles entangle and twist,
A rabbit named Benny can't bear to be missed.
He hops on the vines, makes a game of his flight,
While the berries all chuckle, "What a funny sight!"

The blackbirds sing tunes, quirky and strange,
As the bushes retort, "Let's join in the change!"
A mischievous spider spins webs full of laughs,
While hedgehogs take bets on their acorn graph!

Oh, the tangled paths lead to treasures untold,
With laughter as currency, more precious than gold.
When shadows grow long, and the moon starts to play,
The bramble becomes home to a nighttime ballet.

So skip through the thorns and embrace all the fun,
With friends all around, let the revelry run!
In this wild, prickly wonder, joy never does sway,
In the verses of life in the bramble way!

Songs of the Garden Guardian

Oh, the wise old gnome with a grin of delight,
Plays tunes on his flute every day and night.
He guards all the flowers, the veggies, the weeds,
With a wink and a chuckle, fulfilling their needs.

He dances through petals, steps light as a breeze,
While carrots debate if they're more of a tease.
"Don't underestimate us!" the radishes claim,
As tomatoes just giggle, "We're all in the game!"

The gnome spins a tale of the critters so sly,
"All hail the garden, where laughter can fly!"
The onions would cry, but their tears are of glee,
For the joy in this plot is the best sight to see.

So here's to the guardian, our jester in green,
With jokes on the daisies and laughter unseen.
In this garden of whimsy, come join in the cheer,
With songs of the gnome, let's make it all clear!

A Symposium of Stinging Secrets

In a garden hid from sight,
A plant with spiky crowns took flight.
Whispers shared among the weeds,
Of pranks and pokes, and funny deeds.

With tiny hands they play a game,
A tickle here, a jab, no shame.
The daisies giggle, roses roll,
While naughty greens play their stroll.

Tales of laughter in the sun,
Where rhubarb dances, having fun.
They slap the fool who dares come near,
And share a chuckle with no fear.

So when you tread on leafy ground,
Beware the stingers lurking round.
For nature hides her jests so well,
In a leafy, prickly, secret spell.

Memoirs of the Forgotten Flora

In corners where the shadows crawl,
Forgotten greens have tales to call.
With cups of tea and little bites,
They meet to share their silly nights.

A thistle once wore a jester's hat,
While dandelions danced with a cat.
They spoke of days they'd jostled and spun,
Each flower laughing, just for fun.

Petals whispered of prankish ways,
As ivy tangled in leafy frays.
The lavender laughed, a sweet surprise,
As mushrooms crack jokes in disguise.

So in the thicket where mischief thrives,
Each leaf has stories that come alive.
With every rustle and gentle breeze,
The forgotten flora shares their tease.

The Voice of the Elusive Herb

In shadows deep where laughter lingers,
The herb with wit play tricks with fingers.
A fragrant sage, a humble thyme,
Sing songs of humor, always rhyme.

Oft hiding in the pantry tight,
They chat and chuckle 'til the night.
With every sprinkle, every shake,
They craft their jokes, make no mistake.

"Why did the carrot bring a coat?"
They cackle loud, then start to gloat.
"In case of peas, it's quite absurd,
Just like the voice of this quirky herb!"

So if you seek a laugh or jest,
Just lend an ear, and you'll be blessed.
For in the quiet, herbs will say,
The funniest things in the oddest way.

Stanzas from the Hidden Wilderness

In wilds where the secrets play,
The plants conspire in their own way.
With laughter rising like the dew,
A symphony of green ensues.

A fern cracks jokes from leafy heights,
While moss plots silly, mossy nights.
The wildflowers, with colors bold,
Tell tales of laughs in hues untold.

"Knock, knock!" chirps the sweet pea vine,
"Who's there?" asks the elder, feeling fine.
"A little beet, don't let him in,
He's known for peeling and for spin!"

So, venture forth where greens reside,
In hidden corners, let fun abide.
For nature holds her laughter tight,
A wilderness of joy in sight.

Echoes of the Green Thorn

In the garden where mischief grows,
Prickly plants aim to oppose.
With a scratch and a jump, they play a game,
Even the insects know their name.

A tiny poke, a playful tease,
Famished critters flee with ease.
Laughter blooms where thorns retreat,
Nature's jesters in leafy seat.

Whispers of mayhem in the air,
Ticklish leaves with a spiky flair.
Jumps and giggles fill the space,
In this wild, hilarious place.

So here we dance in nature's jest,
Among green tricks we jest the best.
With every scratch, a story grows,
In this realm where laughter flows.

Tales from the Wild Green

Once I wandered in fields so bright,
Where leaves all chuckled in the light.
Each pointed end had a tale to share,
Of clumsy critters caught unaware.

A squirrel danced, then took a dive,
Into the patch that came alive.
With every jump, a little cry,
As nature's pranks brought laughs nearby.

In tangled paths, we found delight,
Giggling at the cheeky sight.
Plants that poke and plants that tease,
Making merry with the breeze.

So grab your shoes and take a chance,
Join the plants in a silly dance.
Life's too short for worry and strife,
Let's laugh together, that's the life!

The Tickling Touch of Nature

Amidst the bushes, mischief brews,
With every step, green humor ensues.
A playful scratch from leafy vines,
Turns grumps into dance, oh how it shines!

Tiptoe lightly, or don't you dare,
For flora's pranks linger in the air.
Nature's fingers gently poke,
With teasing jabs, it's all a joke.

A giggle here, a chuckle there,
The sprightly breeze lifts every care.
Prickly jokes from plants so sly,
Make even the wise old owls cry!

So dance with joy in grassy fields,
Where laughter blooms, and fun it yields.
Embrace the play, the tickle, the tease,
In nature's game, let's find some ease!

Symphony of Sharp Leaves

In the orchestra of green and gold,
The sharp leaves strum, their stories told.
With a rustle and a cheeky grin,
They poke and prod, let the fun begin!

A leaf plays bass, a thorn plays lead,
While insects jam, oh yes indeed!
With every prick, a note doth sound,
Creating laughter all around.

The melody's wild, a ticklish tune,
Under the watch of a beaming moon.
Join the chorus of nature's maybe,
For life is music that drives us crazy!

So clap your hands and stomp your feet,
In this sharp-symphony, life's a treat.
Let the sharp leaves serenade your heart,
In their playful jest, let's all take part!

The Art of Wild Resistance

In the garden, woes take flight,
A prickly crew with spiky might.
They laugh at rules, oh what a sight,
Waging war on blooms so bright.

Tickled leaves in breezy dance,
Obnoxious weeds in bold romance.
With every stem, they take a chance,
Defying tools, they prance, they prance.

The snippers come with vengeful cheer,
Yet in their grip, they just won't fear.
A tug, a pull, all ends in sneer,
"Come back next year, we'll still be here!"

Laughter echoes through the plot,
Wild things strut, they care not a jot.
Resilience wrapped in a thorny knot,
Flamboyant rebels, they'll never rot.

Rhythms of the Green Underdog

Underfoot, the greens compose,
An unseen beat that gently flows.
With every root, a tale arose,
In nature's dance, the wild things pose.

The sun dips low, the shadows creep,
Silly sprouts begin to leap.
Mischievous roots, they laugh and beep,
In the soil, their secrets keep.

Grasshoppers join, they jump in tune,
While daisies sway to a silly croon.
The lowly weeds, under silver moon,
Nibble on dreams, a wild festoon.

Leaves whisper tales of joy and strife,
In the beat of the green, they find their life.
Nature's orchestra cuts like a knife,
Notes of laughter, free from the rife.

Nature's Thorns and Tenderness

In a patch where wild things grow,
Thorns are friends, as we all know.
With gentle hearts, they steal the show,
While daisies dance in sweet tableau.

Beneath the prickles, hugs abound,
A love for chaos, snugly found.
Each tiny bud a joy unbound,
Resilient joy is nature's sound.

Petals giggle in the breeze,
Tickling weeds with effortless ease.
A world alive with nature's tease,
Underneath branches, life's not a breeze.

In this mess, life finds its thread,
For every thorn has laughter fed.
With every jolt, from roots to head,
Nature's quirks will keep us wed.

The Guise of Garden Mysteries

Underneath the ivy's guise,
Mischief lurks where laughter lies.
In the shadows, wisdom flies,
With every sprout, a new surprise.

Rabbits whisper without a care,
"Who needs paths? There's space to share!"
In tangled vines, they play a dare,
Exploring secrets hidden and rare.

With puns delivered in leafy jest,
Nature plays, and we are blessed.
A wild ensemble, an ongoing quest,
In the garden, who's truly best?

We bask in quirks, an odd parade,
While flowers plan their great charade.
In the wilds where mischief's made,
The jesters dance and never fade.

Serenade in Tangled Growth

In a garden where whimsy twirls,
Dancing weeds give funny swirls,
They poke and prod with playful glee,
Like tiny jesters shouting, "Look at me!"

A leaf lingers with a cheeky grin,
Whispers secrets in leafy sin,
"Why tidy up? Just let it be!"
The chaos is as grand as a jubilee!

The flowers gossip, oh what a tease,
"Did you see that? He pricked his knees!"
A dandelion giggles, makes a fuzz,
In this riot, there's only one buzz!

So come and join this vibrant jest,
With tangled friends, you'll feel the best,
For in this mess, life's joy is rife,
In every prick lies a bit of life!

Tapestry of Thorns and Dreams

A rose with spikes is life's sweet joke,
It whispers softly as you poke,
"Is that a kiss? Or was it a jab?"
In botanical ballet, it's quite a fab!

In the meadow where laughter grows,
Prickly paths in funny rows,
They trip you up, oh what a scene,
As giggles echo between the green!

With dreams woven in tangled threads,
A wild patch upends all the spreads,
Laughter erupts with every stumble,
As nature's foes become our fumble!

So watch your step in this playful dance,
Where thorns and giggles have a chance,
To spread some magic, wild and bright,
In this tapestry, life's pure delight!

Reflections in the Prickled Breeze

In a field where the sharp winds play,
Each bristle wiggles in a merry ballet,
They poke the sun with tiny pings,
Announcing their joy with silly flings!

A chatterbox bush begins to boast,
"I'm sharper than most, come have a toast!"
While daisies snicker, minds intertwined,
In this prickle fest, joy's not confined!

The clouds float by with knowing smiles,
As we dance through terrains, facing trials,
And though we laugh, there's some delight,
In the sways of these prickers, we find our light.

So raise a glass to the jests we weave,
With every sharp note, it's hard to grieve,
For in this laughter, life's tender hush,
Brings us closer in every hush!

Reveries of the Biting Leaf

Oh biting leaf with a waggish grin,
You tickle the toes, let the fun begin!
Your jagged edges hold mischief tight,
In the jumble where laughter takes flight!

With sly appeals and naughty traits,
You tease the passerby, oh such fates!
"What's that? A leaf? Or is it a dare?"
In this game of nature, proceed with care!

The sun beams down as pranks take shape,
In the dance of fools, there's no escape,
For every prick carries whispers and dreams,
In this leafy revelry, nothing is as it seems!

So linger a while in this leafy lounge,
Where jovial spirits and laughter trounce,
For in biting jests lies an artful reprieve,
In the garden of whims, all hearts believe!

Gravitational Green Tales

In a garden where gravity bends,
The flowers tell jokes to their leafy friends.
A tomato trips, falls on its face,
And the broccoli giggles, 'What a disgrace!'

The carrots dance with the juicy peas,
While spinach sings to the buzzing bees.
A cucumber slips on a dew-filled grin,
And the laughter of radishes starts to spin.

A potato jokes, 'I'm really quite starch,
Yet here I am, hugging this damp little larch.'
The blooms all chuckle, they can't help but sway,
In the world where the veggies just love to play.

When evening falls, the moon's so bright,
The plants share tales of their silly plight.
With roots intertwined, they sing out in mirth,
In the garden of giggles, they know their worth.

Veils of Earthly Whispers

Amidst the leaves, a whispering breeze,
Is a gossiping buzz that tickles your knees.
The daisies chortle of gossip well-kept,
While the mossy stones silently crept.

The thistles gossip 'bout the pesky ants,
Who wear little boots doing their dance.
A sneaky snail joins with tales of delight,
'You'll never guess who danced all night!'

The shadows wiggle, and giggles abound,
With every rustle, new jokes are found.
A sly little frog croaks quite a pun,
'The lily pads gleam, oh what a run!'

As the sun sets low and the stars peep through,
Each leaf drops a tale that's fresh and new.
Their soft laughter floats on the cool, night air,
For in nature's comedy, there's always a rare.

The Language of the Entangled

In vines that twist with a curious grace,
A story unfolds in a tangled space.
Where the ivy mocks the wise old oak,
And even the mushrooms join in the joke.

The branches clap in a leafy cheer,
As laughter erupts, oh so sincere.
A willow whispers secrets so sly,
'Why did the hedge grow so high?'

The ferns all chuckle, their fronds flutter wide,
At the antics unveiled on this green hillside.
With roots interwoven in a jolly embrace,
They spin tangled tales in this leafy place.

When the sun dips low, through gaps they peek,
Sharing the punchlines in nature's unique speak.
The laughter resounds, oh what a delight,
In the quirky old woods where humor takes flight.

Echoing Among the Green Shadows

In shadows deep where the green leaves stir,
Whispers of laughter float soft as fur.
A squirrel debates with a wise little bee,
On who's the best jester in their leafy spree.

The thrum of the crickets adds rhythm and rhyme,
As blossoms all giggle, they're having a prime.
A daffodil snickers at a grumpy old sprout,
'You need a good laugh, let go of that pout!'

The moonlight glimmers on the grass so bright,
While owls hoot softly, 'What a silly night!'
The laughter cascades like a gentle stream,
In this garden of shadows, there's joy that beams.

So when you wander where the green things grow,
Join in the fun, let the good vibes flow.
For buried in laughter, the earth does know,
That humor connects us in a warm, gentle glow.

Chronicles of the Garden's Bite

In the garden, plants arise,
Whispers of mischief in disguise.
A prickly patch waits for a fool,
Ouch! That sting breaks all the rules.

A buzzard snickers from a tree,
Gathering all the gossip, you see.
The daffodils chuckle, heads held high,
While daisies laugh and the lilies sigh.

The rabbit hops, a bemused stare,
Dodging the weeds, unaware of the snare.
A prickly situation lurking 'round,
In the garden, laughter is profound.

So watch your step, or you may meet
A spiky fate on your bare feet.
With every shiver, a goofy grin,
In this wild place, the giggles begin.

Secrets in the Underbrush

Beneath the thicket, secrets stew,
Where tiny critters test what is true.
A curious squirrel, with a twitchy nose,
Stumbles 'cross mischief in thorny prose.

The hedgehogs roll, a prickly ball,
Laughing at those who sit and crawl.
The ants march on, so sly and quick,
Unaware their plan is about to stick.

A turtle chuckles at the ruckus,
Why rush when the leaves provide a fuss?
With every crackle, a hidden chortle,
As shadows dance near the garden's portal.

So join the fun, don't mind the prickle,
For humor thrives where nature's fickle.
In every corner, a joke awaits,
Underbrush secrets, the garden's traits.

A Tangle of Verdant Memories

In a tangle of greens and browns,
Tree trunks tell tales like clowns.
The vines twist and shout, in jest,
Whispers of sunlight and a feathered nest.

A mischievous breeze swirls a caper,
As daisies giggle, pulling the paper.
"Who wrote this mess?" the bushes demand,
While curling ferns wave a leafy hand.

The scarecrow sways, with a goofy grin,
While veggies plot how to catch the wind.
With every rustle, a memory spins,
Of laughter stored where the fun begins.

Amongst the weeds, tales intertwine,
Sharing giggles with the sun's fine line.
So gather 'round for a greenish cheer,
In tangled memories, the fun is near.

The Itch Behind the Foliage

Behind the leaves, a tickle resides,
A bubbly laugh where nature hides.
With every scratch and every grin,
The day brings joy where fun begins.

The ladybugs dance on the tips of stems,
While caterpillars plot as they pretend.
"Did you feel that?" whispers the breeze,
As petals giggle in a gentle tease.

A frolicsome fox jumps high and low,
Jesting with weeds that like to grow.
"Can you scratch my back?!" a plant exclaims,
But all the giggles spark secret games.

So wander close, if you dare to peek,
Behind the foliage, laughter speaks.
An itch of joy, a jolly sight,
In nature's world, the mood is bright.

The Verdant Symphony

In the garden where green things grow,
A frog plays a tune, oh so slow,
The flowers are dancing, swaying with flair,
While bees sing loudly, buzzing the air.

The sun beams down in a mischievous way,
Tickling the leaves as they join in the play,
A breeze strolls through with a cheeky grin,
Whispers of laughter where chaos begins.

A snail starts a race, but he won't catch a break,
His finish line's marked by a mischievous snake,
The rabbits just giggle, they won't take a chance,
While the old owl watches, enjoying the dance.

So here in this glade, each creature is bold,
Life's a grand party, with tales to be told,
Nature's bright orchestra, hilarious and free,
Tunes of the wild, where we all can agree.

Footsteps in the Thicket

Through the bushes, a rustle, what do I see?
A raccoon with snacks, as happy as can be,
He stumbles and fumbles, drops chips on the ground,
In the twilight whispers, his munching sounds round.

At dusk, the owls hoot their comical tune,
While crickets join in, a wild cartoon,
The shadows go shimmying, shapes in the dark,
As fireflies twinkle, lighting the park.

A mischievous squirrel leaps, oh what a sight,
Falling on branches, he gives quite a fright,
But he shrugs it off, with a flick of his tail,
Laughing at all, he won't ever fail.

In this thicket where chaos reigns,
Every rustling leaf plays hilarious games,
With footsteps of joy in the woods so thick,
Nature's own circus, full of its tricks.

Woven Tales of Wilderness

In the bramble where the wild things thrive,
A chameleon hides, trying to jive,
He slips on a leaf, with a sliding surprise,
And turns a bright orange, what a wild guise!

The badger is busy, digging with glee,
Finding lost treasures beneath the old tree,
But what does he find, a shoe and a hat?
"Oh no! Not my size!" he shakes his head flat.

A fox cracks a joke to a curious hare,
Who chuckles and snorts, barely gets air,
While overhead, a crow caws out loud,
"Did you hear that one? I'm drawing a crowd!"

These tales of the wild, outlandish and bright,
Woven in laughter from morning to night,
In the heart of the woods, the stories unfold,
Where humor and nature are boldly retold.

Hidden Dances of the Wild

In the shadows of ferns, the fox takes a chance,
Twisting and turning, he joins in the dance,
With butterflies fluttering, all colors and hues,
They swirl and they twirl, without any dues.

A turtle joins in, though he moves quite slow,
He shimmies and shakes, putting on a show,
The beetles all giggle, break into a roll,
While the winds play a tune, they let go and stroll.

With crickets conducting from under a log,
The frogs leap and croak, "We're the party rogues!"
Each step is a blast, each leap full of joy,
In hidden wild dances, nature's own ploy.

So let's celebrate nature, whimsical and free,
In the secretive spots where we laugh with glee,
These hidden performances hide wild surprise,
In the heart of the woods, where humor lies.

Whispers from the Thorned Grove

In the grove where prickers play,
Laughter dances through the day.
With each poke, a silly shout,
Who knew thorns could bring about?

Amidst the greens, a giggle grows,
A tickle here, a jab that flows.
Watch your step, or you'll surely find,
A funny tale that's unconfined.

The buzzing bugs join in the cheer,
As thorns enact a prank so clear.
Innocent games of poke and prod,
Nature's jesters, oh so odd.

So come and join this merry fest,
Where even prickles love to jest.
With each rub, a chuckle rides,
In this grove where humor hides.

Symphony of Stinging Shadows

In shadows deep where laughter stings,
A symphony of humor springs.
The bushes chuckle, branches tease,
Each scratch brings giggles with the breeze.

When night descends and critters creep,
The thorns start humming, not a peep.
A harp of sharpness strums so bright,
Echoes of laughter fill the night.

A dance of prickles, oh what a sight,
With every jab, we laugh in fright.
The moon observes this merry plight,
As shadows prickle with delight.

So let the thorns embrace the fun,
In every poke, a pun begun.
A symphony composed of glee,
In stinging shades, we all agree.

Echoes in the Wild Green

In wild green where whispers blend,
Amidst the thorns, the laughs extend.
A poke, a prod, a friendly jest,
In nature's arms, we find our best.

The echoes ring, a fun refrain,
In prickly patches, joy sustains.
With every brush against the leaves,
A chuckle shared, the spirit weaves.

The grass sways with a knowing grin,
As thorns conspire, let the games begin.
In this wild so lush and bright,
We'll weave our jokes from day to night.

So come join in the playful spree,
Where echoes laugh in harmony.
Within the greens, hilarity blooms,
In thorny realms, joy surely looms.

Ballad of the Prickly Scribe

In a land where pokes create the lore,
A scribe with thorns loves to explore.
With every jab, a tale unfolds,
Of mindful laughs and prickle holds.

He writes of woes with a vicious quill,
Each prick a story, a quirky thrill.
The paper scratched—a wild delight,
In a ballad from the thorny night.

Beware the tales that twist and turn,
Where every poke is a lesson learned.
In scribbled lines, a chuckle stays,
As laughter weaves through prickle plays.

So gather 'round and heed the call,
Of the scribe whose thorns can enthrall.
In the world of jests and witty vibes,
The ballad rolls, the humor thrives.

Pulses of Untamed Growth

In a garden of wild delights,
I tangle with my feet in the nights,
Forgot my shoes just for a spree,
Now my toes dance with glee.

A patch of green went for a stroll,
Curious hands can take a toll,
With each brush, a tickle, a laugh,
Nature's way of having a gaffe.

They waved their leaves, a cheeky grin,
Inviting me to join their din,
I laughed and rolled, embraced the scene,
In this green chaos, I'm the queen!

So here's to growth that bites and teasing,
Life's little pricks are quite appeasing,
We dance with plants, both proud and spry,
In this bloom of fun, oh my, oh my!

The Push and Pull of Green

Green tugged my shirt, said 'Come and play!'
I laughed and replied, 'Not today!'
But with each tug and every sweep,
I fell in love with weeds that creep.

They wrapped around my ankles tight,
With vines that shouted, 'What a sight!'
Pulling me closer, to frolic and spin,
Who would've guessed they'd invite me in?

My garden grows in fits and starts,
With leafy jokes that warm my heart,
Each push and pull, a fun charade,
In this green world, I'm quite the blade!

Tickles from the creeping vine,
Fuzzy leaves, oh how they shine,
A tug of war that's rather grand,
In the cheers of the muddled land!

Blossoms of the Heart's Denial

In petals bright, I pick my fight,
With blooms that dance in the twilight,
Each color winks, a sly romance,
While I just giggle, take a chance.

Denial blooms like weeds in spring,
With witty jabs, they poke and sing,
I duck and weave through rose-thorn gates,
Laughing at my heart's debates!

Flowers say, 'Come, don't be shy!'
But I'm too busy saying bye,
To crush or caress, that's the riddle,
With every petal, life's a fiddle!

Yet in this game of push and shove,
The blossoms tease me, tough love,
So here I sway, a blushing fool,
In the garden of my heart's own school.

Interludes of Spiky Serenity

In the quiet, spiky things play,
With ticklish whispers, come what may,
I sit in peace, a throne of thorns,
Amid the laughter, my joy adorns.

Nature's pincushion, oh so raw,
It gives a poke with every flaw,
Yet here I find a quirky charm,
A tickle here can do no harm.

A couple of jabs, then comes the giggle,
In nature's orchestra, I dance and wiggle,
Soft and sharp, a duo so rare,
In interludes, I breathe fresh air.

So let the spikes keep up their tease,
I'm here to laugh, be wild, and seize,
In spiky serenity, I'm free,
With every prickle, joy's the key!

Navigating the Wild Hedge

In the thicket, where secrets creep,
A squirrel plots for lunch—what a leap!
While I dodge thorns in a wobbly gait,
I swear these bushes mock my fate.

Laughter rings as bees buzz by,
Dandelions join in, oh my oh my!
Each step a dance, each thorn a cheer,
The wild hedge whispers, 'Have no fear!'

Found a treasure: a rogue pair of socks,
What's that? A raccoon in flip-flop mocks?
In this chaos, I trip and twist,
Life's a joke; I can't resist!

So here I stand in leafy embrace,
With foliage friends, I find my place.
Through tangled paths, I chuckle loud,
In the wild hedge, I'm utterly proud.

The Dance of the Unyielding

Two weeds in a ramble, footloose and free,
Challenging folks to a dance-off spree.
With roots in the soil, they boogie around,
Each twist and turn makes the ground shake and sound.

"Oh dear neighbor," the thistle proclaimed,\n"Your dance moves are wild, but I'm unashamed!
I'll twist you around with a twist of my stem,
With each spin and whirl, I'll take down your gem!"

Laughter erupts from the daisies nearby,
While the grass joins in—a wild, wacky high!
As petals go flying and thorns take a twirl,
Even the bugs join this dance of the pearl.

So if you're feeling heavy, just pop on a leaf,
Join the dance of the wild; it's the ultimate relief.
In unyielding fun, we find our way,
Together we sway, come what may!

Minted Moments of Wildness

In the garden of giggles, where herbs dream big,
A sprig of mint sings with a wobbly jig.
"I'm cooler than ice, and twice as neat,"
Says the mint, while the basil taps its feet.

Chasing after herbs, I skip down the lane,
With parsley and thyme, let's go insane!
They giggle and wiggle, making me grin,
When did a chef's garden turn into a din?

Come smell the laughter, oh can you smell?
Each fresh little sprout has a story to tell.
With roots intertwined and stories so potent,
This patch of wildness is purely an omen.

So let's be fresh, let's be bold as we play,
In the minted moments, we seize the day.
With each whiff of whimsy, we take a chance,
In this herbal dance, we'll forever prance!

Unfurling Tales of Wild Roots

Where roots intertwine, a tale begins,
Of rascally plants and their playful sins.
With whispers of laughter beneath the ground,
Each story unravels, a joy to be found.

The willow speaks softly, with sass and delight,
"I once dressed a frog in a leafy nightlight!"
While the pine chuckles, "Oh do tell more,
Of those silly bugs that just can't ignore!"

From tendrils and twirls, the tales take flight,
With each twist and turn, laughter ignites.
The daisies whisper, "Let's not be shy,
In the garden of wildness, we're all clouds to fly!"

So come join the chorus, the roots call your name,
In the stories of wildness, oh, what a game!
As we unfurl together, with glee in our roots,
Life's a whimsical dance, in our leafy suits!

Secrets of the Emerald Forest

In the forest where giggles grow,
Trees whisper secrets, oh so low.
Mushrooms dance in polka-dot glee,
Birds tell jokes, whoopee! Whoopee!

Squirrels wear hats made of leaves,
Chasing each other, oh how they tease!
Rabbits hop, their tails a blur,
While owls roll eyes, what a stir!

Acorns chuckle as they tumble down,
Frogs croak tales, wearing crowns from town.
The sun giggles, peeking through,
Tickling plants, making them dew!

So, if you wander, be light on your feet,
In this playful place, joy is sweet.
Laughter echoes as you roam free,
In this emerald land, come play with me!

Lament of the Hidden Stinger

In the garden lies a tale so bold,
Of prickly creatures, oh if told!
Buzzing bees, with such a sting,
Freely laughing—oh what a fling!

The tiny ones, with stripes of delight,
Flaunting their giggles in middle of flight.
"Watch your step!" they loudly shout,
As I hop around, not wanting to pout.

A dance of woe, the thorns do swoon,
They prick my toes—oh, how they croon!
Yet in their jab, a humor resides,
Roll with the punches, enjoy the rides!

Under the leaves, the hidden grins,
Greet all the pain with chuckles and spins.
So here's to the stinger, a cheeky sprite,
Who shows us laughter, in every bite!

Verses in the Verdant Underbrush

In the underbrush, where the oddballs play,
Frogs in tuxedos hop night and day.
Vines sneak up to tickle your toes,
While weeds gossip under their bows.

A rabbit plays tricks, oh what a sight,
Wearing a wig, looking just right.
Hedgehogs giggle, rolling with glee,
As they plan a surprise garden tea!

The sun peeks in with a cheeky grin,
Making shadows dance, where fun begins.
Bumblebees belt out a jazzy refrain,
As worms wiggle wiggly, like they're insane!

So join the party in green, take a chance,
In this wild place, let's all dance.
Laughter blooms in every nook,
Every plant tells tales, just take a look!

The Language of the Wild Weeds

Oh, what a language the weeds do speak,
In their leafy way, so playful and chic.
With winks and nudges, they share their lore,
"Stay for a chat, we've so much in store!"

They murmur softly, like whispers of green,
Telling wild tales of all they've seen.
"Watch your step, don't trip on our pride!
We're more than a bother, come join the ride!"

With laughter sprouting from every stem,
Secrets unfold—oh, what a gem!
A wild party where chuckles grow wide,
In this garden of glee, let's all abide.

So grab your boots, come poke around,
In a world where fun and laughter abound.
The weeds want to share in their cheeky way,
Join the wild laughter, and stay for a play!

www.ingramcontent.com/pod-product-compliance
Lightning Source LLC
Chambersburg PA
CBHW051632160426
43209CB00004B/613